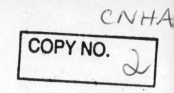
Elves in the Wainscotting

Joe Sheerin was born in Ireland in 1941. He is the author of *A Crack in the Ice* (1984) and his work has also appeareed in Faber's *Poetry Introductions* (1982) and in the Oxford*Poets Anthology* (2000).

Also by Joe Sheerin

A Crack in the Ice

JOE SHEERIN

Elves in the Wainscotting

Oxford*Poets*

CARCANET

First published in Great Britain in 2002 by
Carcanet Press Limited
4th Floor, Conavon Court
12–16 Blackfriars Street
Manchester M3 5BQ

A CIP catalogue record for this book
is available from the British Library

ISBN 1 903039 61 4

The publisher acknowledges financial assistance
from the Arts Council of England

Set in Monotype Garamond by XL Publishing Services, Tiverton
Printed and bound in England by SRP Ltd, Exeter

With no little gratitude to Dennis O'Driscoll
for
his faith and charity over the years

Contents

Medical Advice

Kisses shorten life; mixing strange spittle
Or sucking in microbes, dozing under small flaps
Of gum or carelessly grazing on the plankton
Of teeth upsets the ecology of the mouth.

One could, of course, wear a surgical mask
And agree not to exhale while gauze touched
Gauze, or write letters from a distance
Disinfecting the pen and using self
Sealing envelopes for safety.

Some, I know, blinded by passion shed their
Clothes like children, pressing nakedness
To nakedness, making contact at all points
Throwing caution to the wind or worse.

A few die early from inhaled infection that
Turns plump hearts into prunes before their
Time, that withers the skin and blanks the
Brightness of the eye. They are love's martyrs.

Others with strong constitutions survive. Nursing
Injuries like war wounds, they limp through
Marriage, frequently resting on the shoulders
Of their love, while the cautious live to a ripe old
Age, camouflaging internal bleeding as late periods.

Photofit

I was leaving the supermarket with
Two bags bloated with things that
Wilt and wither and rot into dark pools
Of themselves if not consumed on the
Journey home or shortly thereafter,

When a policemen in plain clothes and
Looking like a neighbour stopped me,
To show a photograph furtive as a dirty
Postcard displaying a man's head, face on
And side view and marked off in geometric
Shapes. I averted my eyes but he egged me
On, suggesting perhaps I saw him in a pub
Or club, a restaurant or cinema, at a place
Of work, boarding a bus, waiting in a
Butcher's queue, lurking near a school crossing.

In truth I recognised him but bit by bit,
The eyes from somewhere, the nose from somewhere
Else, the glisten of his lips in my wife's
Kissing; the shape of the face was my own.
The hair line brought back a sepia photograph
In a drawer. 'Arrest everyone', would be insolence,
Although I saw the sadness in his face.

I had stood too long in the sun and as I
Walked home my food dribbled around my feet
Like a bad conscience.

A Small Demonstration

In the butcher's shop with the rabbits
And the pheasants and the turkeys and the
Split pigs were the babies, spread out
On slabs face downwards like circus
Midgets weary after a day's performance.

It's not native child-meat, the butcher,
His face and hands pale with grief, explained
Not wishing to offend our sensibilities as the day
Was bitter enough to hone a dull conscience.

They came from another country and they
Died humanely. He turned one over with
A stevedore's hook and sure enough the
Face, soft as a putto, was transfixed
In a cheeky grin from ear to ear. We gasped,

Believing the trade of butchery with its
Bloodied troughs and hooks and cleaving knives
Was cruel as gall, but here limb-perfect a child
No bigger than our own smiled at us from between
The parsley of familiar rabbit and fowl.

It was a time for decision. We counted
Small change like misers in the hungry
Mouths of purses, reading their value in braille.
Just then the demonstrators arrived; turkey
Farmers and rabbit breeders from the country
Bearing placards like sharpened staves and
Begging us for the love of gentle Jesus to
Think on their thin children pining at home.

Ciné Vérité

At the ringing of a Hollywood death bell
our tears trained like saliva gather
behind our eyes. Even the rising damp on
the wall behind us peels its paper showing
a heart of stone softened by long watching.

This is the lather of soap opera to
cleanse the emotions with salt water.
We have seen it before and swallowed
the familiar lump that cheap literature
raises in our throat before bed and the
reassurance of warm flesh raises the living.

Now in truth a real young girl is dying
frail as a crone, bent double in a hospital
bed, her mother holding a begging dish
for mercy's coins to buy a life gadget so
that some mother's child will rise
like an angel from the covers full-cheeked.

When the television has gasped and gathered
in its light to a diamond point we ascend
the stairs to find no answers in the easy persuasion
of thighs, but touch prudishly aware of the unwanted
camera watching at the angle of the wall.

Honeymood

John and Jane are going on their
Honeymood. Their two cases swollen
With unused details lounge in the

Belly of the plane. They have a
Seat near the window overlooking
A fragile wing. The plane rises,

Above an aerial postcard of houses and
Streets and toy cars until the clouds
Receive them into a thinly veiled bed of mist.

Flying blind, thrust and terror cause
A sharp intake of breath. Turbulence pips
The ears and nudges tummies playfully,
Sharing a secret. Out in the sun

Light above clouds countless as sheep
Grazing on a mountain that's no longer
There, they both smile. A stewardess

Treading the corridor like Blondin smiles
Too. Jane is still wearing her veil.

The Jailors of Icarus

There's no way they could of got
Out of here. Them walls at least
Twenty foot high and smooth, not to
Mention the barbs set on the top.
And poisoned. It's a bloody mystery.

What'll we tell the gaffer when he
Come round to do the inspection?
We can't tell him they flew out.
They're not fucking birds, are they?

It's a bloody mystery and it's the
High jump for us if we can't come up
With an explanation. Stamp on the
Ground for tunnels. Look under straw
For hidden spades. Check for melted ice.

I've been through all that, and there's no
Way they could of got out. But they're
Not here. They must of sprouted friggin
Wings and the gaffer will hardly wear that.

They looked dumbly skyward pleading
To Heaven for help. Hot wax like errant
Raindrops stung their faces.

Heroics

Hercules diverted a river. Old Sheerin
Laboured with a graip every day and
Never finished a pyramid of rank dung.

Horses that bared their teeth in
Resentment ploughed his land. The flesh
He fed them on blistered his hands.

He drove thin nimble cattle, wild
As hares, to a fair and sold them
For a song in the great depression.

Men could not imagine lions on those
Small Northern hills. Instead he slew foxes,
Cutting their tongues out for small rewards.

Each year he nourished a long-bodied pig
Into autumn and killed it. We hid from
The blast of its scream behind rain barrels.

When the iron-beaked crows, wheeling dark
Against a low sky, raided his fields,
He shot some leaving them rotting on sticks.

He led a gaunt heifer, wide-eyed as
A bride, to a sullen short-legged
Bull and prayed to the gods of fertility.

Wooing a proud woman in her
Blossoming youth, he started a war
Bloodless but no less fierce for all that.

He hung acid apples from the rafters
And watched them dodge around our ripe
Cheeks holding the sky up laughing.

He pitted his patience against hares
In the snow, tracking them for hours
And returning with a golden carcase to eat.

Wading waist deep in the marshes of a lake
He fished for perch, hacking their greedy
Heads off when they swallowed the hook.

He dug graves for bodies he knew
Spading soil out across his head
Fearless, his two feet in Hades.

Twelve labours behind him and still
Wondering if the gods had forgiven him,
Never having completed any one of them.

The Soothsayer

I had my fortune told by a gypsy with
A stethoscope. I expected a crystal ball,
A black cat or tarot cards at least.

Instead she sat in a desked room and wore
A white coat. A bottle of fresh blood and
A few gallstones littered her desk.

She assured me as she took my pulse that
The blood recently taken could save death.
The gallstones she kept as trophies.

I undressed to a singlet preserving my
Dignity with my hand. She listened to me
Back and front. I coughed and she looked

Grave. I dressed and asked my fortune.
She said I would soon be meeting a dark
Stranger. It was an inauspicious time
For love and I would need some money.

A Ghost's Life

The maximum age of a house ghost is
Five hundred years. After that they
Pack their shrouds and fuck off
To other places without walls or

Stairways or hedges or sunken lawns.
They've done their porridge, floating
Across old ground, bending over cots,
Fading through walls and making hackles
Rise with their behind presence.

Perhaps then they go to factories, sit
Under groaning pipes, pass through lathes,
And sulk in cold canteens until sun-up;
Or hang over railway bridges like tramps,
Or spit into rivers, or loiter outside
Closed shops, until the first bus pierces
The dawn; then fade silent as darkness.

What happens then is pure speculation. Some
Say they return, hitch a likely spermatozoon,
Steer it to an egg, sit at anchor, make eyes,
Sprout limbs of blood, kick the hostess
Mischievously from the inside, butt
Downwards with the head, break out, scream.

Loki

The god of mischief rules. He sends some,
Without minds, roaring through corridors,
Careering against chairs, crashing foreheads
Against brick. They laugh like thunder and only
Ever threaten to use their cocks in anger.

Young women, equipped like Venus, are
As open as petticoats. They dribble smiles
And stroke their thighs; or expose tits
They can never hang an infant on.

Other with minds as nimble as music, he
Imprisons in diseased bodies that wither
From the toes to the neck. The heads
Are the last to die, helpless as rabbits.
They know the gentleness of hand on
Breast and the love that passes understanding.

He removes the spines of some children
In the womb and mocks others in play
Grounds, legs laden like scrapyards.
He pokes out eyes and bites off tongues
And twists heads round to face the shoulder.

Of course we fight him with drugs and
Callipers and prayers and talking dogs and Health
Acts and toilets chromed like thrones. But he
Always wins again with some new trickery.

Oedipus

Caught between the fear of storm and
The shame of discovery he went inevitable
As a prophecy to his mother's bed,

For the untamed night lashed the panes
And the great maned trees outside plunged
Into the waves of the storm. Unsexed as an
Angel, in a long nightshirt he lay beside her.
It was a night to break houses. The roof
Threatened to part company from the wall-plate
And the foundations groaned at the enormity

Of their task, as all night her knee like
A fallen joist rested on his back, while
Outside the thunder clashed like warriors
And the needles of lightning blinded his eyes.

Magus

It being the time of year for portents
And the night sky brazen in its nakedness
I studied the stars for signs of favour.

So many; some dead as yesterday and
Some crowing their daybreak from the
Silence of deep space. Everywhere light
Eyes blinking promise of a million babes
Swaddled like small mummies in a million wards.

I need one only, brighter than the others
And travelling somewhere. My camel waits
Patiently at the hedge and the pungent
Myrrh in my holdall seeps into the night.

Longing makes the eyes visionary; the
Heavens cartwheel and then return. I would
Settle for earthly wonders now, a unicorn
Prancing from the shadows, answering my call.

For a moment a passing aeroplane looks
Promising, circling and near, then
Gliding to earth behind the hills. It is
Not a night for miracles. I slap my camel
Skyward like Pegasus and myrrh my face
Hoping to surprise love sleeping.

Green Experiences

Nobody likes the Irish. I know,
I have been caught once or twice
Myself hacking at my own shins
Until the gore flowed like cud.

Dressed in a city suit and looking
Serious, I curse the weather. This
Is pardonable and passes for conversation,
Having first forked my tongue with scissors
And spat the blunt bits out, until
My speech like a magpie could repeat
The few things people say with accuracy.

I decoded cricket and found a team worthy
Of support, studied gardening books like
Set texts, hit on a suitable regiment for
My grandfather, changed my name to Smith.

It is all in vain at times. Trapped by pride
I show my colours, forecasting the weather
Coming by the low glide of a swallow.

Hospital Visit

The world ended for my mother
Half-way through an ordinary morning,
A nurse noticing no movement of the
Feather near her mouth called a doctor,

An expert in these matters, who duly
Pronounced her dead, hearing no trickle
Of blood from the metal on her breast.

I arrived late at the dismal hospital
Dull bricked and echoing like a cathedral
With my clattering feet, that accompanied
My undead spirit to the river of loss.

Having lived this moment so often in books
I knew my part, spoke in a low voice like
A girl and let my vision, blurred with tears,
Fix on a filing cabinet while the matron spoke

And handed her effects over in a bag: a dress,
An overcoat, a bundle of letters, a few photographs.
The stained dressings of the wound that had
Been her last years, I couldn't bear to touch.

The Lover

Early in Spring my father went courting
Death's daughter. He shaved a blush
Into his thin jaw, slyly went for walks
Alone at dusk. We observed them dimly
Behind hedges, heard them whisper in the barn.
His face was damp and his meat often lay
Untouched on his plate. We sensed romance.

Hurtful after his solid faithfulness; his stubbled
Kisses and his quiet words were sacraments
(Love had his small-meshed net about our house then),
Not easily spat out or reneged on in the night.

Exhausted from watching we dozed inevitably
And he eloped into the blustery night with
No moon and the scutching wind on his thin
Nightdress. He woke up deceived. In a single

Bed in a dark church I saw him last lying. A candle
Winked and I recognised her passionless eye
And her hair wisping like roots around the pillows.

That night I kissed my children greedily, held
My wife close, promised love for ever. An old
Vow. Somehow, by God, I meant to keep it.

Burying

Buried him deep as clay and stone
Would allow the hacking spades of men who
Knew the land and could gauge six feet
With a wind-washed eye. Let him lie

There mounded; for extra security place
A heavy cross of granite and tramp the
Clay down with brutal feet. Bless your face
Goodbye and clean your boots on the lank
Grass. Auf Wiedersehen, until we meet, echoing
The practised words of the petticoated priest.

He comes back, not sheeted like a ghost
Or rattling chains, or grinning with hair
And stagnant flesh about the skull but large
As life and smiling, one hand in his pocket,
With his hat pulled down and standing at
The dresser. It's morning and the cows are dry.

He has all the wisdom now of the other
Side and your words are cleaned glass –
He can read the schoolboy writing in
Your mind and there's nothing you can say.

This is the resurrection and the second life they spoke of.
Each time two die, only one stays down.

The Christening

For the christening everybody came,
Singly, in pairs and groups, by bus and moped,
Train and car, smiling. They bore gifts,
Silver spoons and chrome mugs, small
Shiny Bibles and brightly painted toys.

We took their coats, for it was winter
And heaped them up on our bed, heavy
Wool and imitation fur and skins of small
Rodents only yesterdead and leather
Stripped from the backs of spermed bulls.

The adoration followed. I wheeled the baby
Out, a small round face in a nest of
Eiderdown. More than a universe of faces
And hands reached down the light years
Of experience to touch his buttery skin.

His mother pats her tummy conscious
Of the recent vacancy and the part
I played is plain as evidence in the
Oily hands of an unscrupulous lawyer.

They made sounds. Gurglings; old wives
In the throes of love and primeval
Grunts; cave men after a full meal
And the cave wall hung with skins and
The antlers like bushes on the floor.

God wisely gave him no sight to see the years
Of his life standing in tiers around him,
The faces that tell stories in short lines.
He is the chance for all of us to start again.

We gave him a name with water. He cried
And when we called, coaxing and pulling in the silk
Threads of ownership, he never turned his head.

We said our thanks and shook each hand by
Name, promised photographs and a girl next time.
Alone, we washed up first and then replaced him
In his cot, carefully as a completed jigsaw.

A Cup of Tea

After months of silence my neighbour knocked.
I presented my eye interrogatively at the peep
Hole and waited. My child, she said, is dead.
I was cagey, aware it might only be a ruse
To open a conversation. Which one? My eyebrow
A horizontal question mark. The one with golden
Hair, blue enamel eyes and porcelain cheeks.
Prove it, I demanded. My kettle was boiling over.

She demagnified and I measured some tea into a pot.
Again she knocked and I offered my eye. True
She held an infant but hard to ascertain whether
Sleeping or dead. I am a cautious person. I
Ordered a mirror and a feather to be brought.
She offered feather and mirror to his lips.
It was a blustery day and I couldn't be sure.
Tickle him, remembering how a tickled child
Twitches in sleep. He made no movement. I
Wasn't convinced. More, more. Under the armpit.

She played walkie-round-the-garden and this-
Little-piggy with his rigid limbs. No smile
Broke the piety of his face. He's dead I conceded.
What am I to do, she asked? A sculptured tear
On her face. Call a doctor and get a death
Certificate. You will need this for the Registrar
Of Deaths. Inform an undertaker stipulating a small
Coffin. You have a choice of consecrated ground or
A crematorium. Contact tax or social security or both.

My tea was drawn and she, I suppose, went home.
I could have set a precedent and asked her in
But she has seven more children and my own
Flesh was dying even as she spoke.

Mind Wandering

Old Sheerin went to Chicago riding a
Bronco ship, uncertain as Brendan, across
The uneven moorlands of the sighing ocean.

Chicago met him like thunder. Trains and
Trams roared into the terminus of his brain.
Cars glided between the cliffs of houses and
The ladies wore furs and tight fitting hats.

His debts paid off he returned, pale as
A cleric, strange among the small hedges
And pencilled fields reclaimed with green dollars.

The rain mellowed his suit and unpolished
His shoes. He opened horses' mouths again and
Felt for lumps in the udders of skittish cattle.

In the silence of turf-cutting it all came
Back. The high banks were skyscrapers, their
Windows darkened and the doors ready to burst.
The peat he wheeled out in a Model-T.

Early Carvings

Those primitives understood the man,
Eyes gouged, a beaked nose and a mouth
Splitting the face like a new moon.

The body square and defensive with
Two stumpy arms; gingerbread legs set apart
Supporting the great bulk of body and head.

The cock is a branch lopped off,
A happy fault in the timber, gazing
Skywards, a challenge to the rest
Pointing earthwards, preparing to rot.

From the side just nose and cock,
Pointing downwards and upwards, one
Smelling out danger, the other ignoring it.

The Old House

It was a mean and cruel house roofed with
Leaky sentiment: the walls white-faced and
Here and there the faded green and yellow tears
Of the rain. The door, half open, did not hinder
Or invite, and between the stone floor and
The smoke-flaked ceiling the wind loitered

Unsure of which way to blow. It was a
Hungry house; the dead came down the steep
Stairs slithering in their coffins and
The cracked cup of holy water was bitter
As salt on the faces of people who knew too
Much truth for their wise tongues to speak.

It was a house of lies. Strident as a prophet
In small things it had enough dark spidery
Corners to trap and hide a man's soul from
Light, to cocoon babies and mummify the
Passions of things that were never said.

The people who haunted it, son after father
Spellbound, dreamt sometimes of ships and spires
Wistfully. When things got too bad someone
Sang a song, or read an almanac, or sighed,
Or prayed, or moved up the tall stairs to bed.

Backcloth

The day I left home it showered. Some from
Clouds and some from under brows heavy as
Thunder. An oblique sun lit my departure
And picked out autumn on the declining trees.

A bit-part actor for so long the lead was
Too onerous. I fluffed my lines and lacked
Stage presence, ducking into the car without
Taking a final bow the audience didn't expect.

Still the backcloth was good, the small
House and the dog and the rutted lane
Fixed in time and the old female figure
(Was it the mother?) forever wiping her nose.

Alter Id

Growing wary of everyone my suspicions
Finally came to rest on myself.

At night I study my face in the mirror
For tell-tale signs of deceit.

Blood on the gums a sure augury
Of a heart on the threshold of breaking.

A tired or sloping tongue can only mean
The kiss of life administered or received.

Moist lips are a presage of hope. The groom
Leading the bride to the parting gate.

My cunning eyes avoiding my own gaze
Show a guilty conscience an urge to run.

I check for pink smudges on the bridge of the nose
An *au revoir* planted in a doorway on tiptoe.

Phone numbers on newspaper margins or small
Talismans are signs that things are not what they seem.

Finally I go through my pockets for double
Bus tickets, theatre stubs, motel match books.

I find dust and small change only. There is nothing yet
To turn suspicion to fact. But I need watching.

Beatitudes

Having everything except love
and money I count my blessings
on the fingers of both hands.

First there are the trees that kiss
cheeks and shake their flounced petticoats.
I bend one little finger to the palm.

For the fliers that unzip the slinks of night
and the bullfinch that dresses up the morning;
two more fingers make half a fist.

Another one is the sight of horses streaming,
the index, the trigger happy, the bachelor, the wind
finder, the Don Juan, the explorer, the reader in the dark.

The luxury of green silence. I count this
on the stubby thumb, the pipe's tamp
the bell push, the inside nipple, the counter of notes.

One fist made I lower my sights
to the left hand, the sinister side. I count
now the misfortunes of my neighbour.

Abbey

After one thousand years the Abbey
is returning itself to the hills, a stalagmite
of shaped stone melting back into the earth.

The trees are knocking on the open door
of the chapel and the grass is walking up the aisle
to the high altar. One sapling a camouflaged intruder
has perched itself impossibly on a shelf
of wall thirty feet up surveying the change.

In the silence of the evening we are
the only worshippers. It is easy at this pious hour
to recall the centuries of celebration,
matins and lauds and vespers day after day.
Even the stones should have learned worship.

This is a little like love giving and turning
back into itself and returning to the place it came from
undiminished but different and always needing
to start again fresh dug from the ruins.

And you a fresh novice might come
breathtaking out of the broken but still holy
chapel apologising for being late as usual.

Lovebirds

The common sparrow or a starling
first brought a cluster of faces to
the kitchen window. A thrush stopped
a heartbeat. A robin, always new,
made us long for his curious return.

Wishing like lovers for lovers' company
we joined societies, bought books and powerful
telescopes, became the peeping Toms
of woodpeckers and jays and nesting owls.

We lay in the grass all day to court
a pipit or tiptoed home at dawn from
strange woods where night jars
rode the darkness on their speckled wings.

A faint hope sent us breathless by car
or train, O love us, O love us, we called
to a Siberian crane out in the mud flats.
Marry me, marry me, harlequin, we
pleaded into the vagrant wind.

We kept diaries as full of secrets
as schoolgirls, recording trysts that promised
so much and ended in a sigh of wings leaving.

That was last year's passion now as stale
as old bread. We have tired of one-way love.
Today I wouldn't cross the road for a phoenix.

Pleasure Seekers

There are some who love old buildings; cathedrals
Are a favourite, the long aisled walk from the salt font
To the high altar and the broken heart of stained glass.

Underfoot the flat memory of dead merchants' families,
Old men, buxom wives and Tom Thumb children, now rest
Where placenta becomes clay and tongues no longer
Wag in the tight ground. Their very taste is in the air.

About the walls, Bishops and Knights incorruptible as
Alloy rest on their elbows and ladies with the rise
Of perfect breasts recline under the decency of bronze.

The recent dead stick to the walls like burrs, the dates
Of their departure too close for comfort while the candelabra
With its lisping light invites a penny for our thoughts.

Others have enough of death and its maudlin glory
And walk past into the bright day. Their pleasure

Only the sudden shock of tenanted beach, the holy
Salt of lips, the perfect dune of an arse.

Genesis

Make more cats said Mrs God
Not toads rats spiders snakes.
Make more swans not vultures
Hawks buzzards eagles kites.
But come in for your tea first.

At the bottom of Eden in a potting shed
He quickly kneaded a clay cat and swan
Blew on them and shut the door tight.

They ate ambrosia and honey from gold
Plates. Afterwards he helped with the washing up.

Finding a white neck speckled with blood
And a cat badly winged and given up
For dead she asked, Is this your idea

Of a joke? He went quiet and distant
The way gods do and wondered if they
Would ever make a go of it, she
Being such a perfectionist.

Local Historian

The chronicler of the street is at last as blind
as Homer. Falls of opaque water now
curtain her eyes. Once her sight could
pierce walls at night, x-ray souls through overcoats.

She watched it all, an Eve with an apple
in her apron pocket and a workman kneeling
to bite it. She smoothing his temples.

She saw Helen stolen while a husband
worked away. Wearing high heeled shoes and
bending to put her two suitcases in the boot
of his car. For a moment she understood why.

She saw a man who was born to duty and should
know better abdicate leaving his well-tended
kingdom and subjects for someone else. And exile.

She watched the war to end all wars fought
over thirty years ending in a long hearse and tears.

She watched a man's Waterloo of emphysema,
a soldier shrunk now to a fist, bent double
grasping for air. His meek wife now becomes
a general, with polished gaiters and gold
epaulettes and a staff car at her disposal.

At night she heard the drone of bombs that
fell at random scattering families to smithereens.
Like the rest she hid in a cupboard holding
her head. In the morning or the following day
or maybe a week after she noted the carnage.

She watched the priest baptising with one hand
and closing the eyelids of the dead with the other.
And a lover kissing one set of lips and fondling another.
And two struggling up the frosty pavement
loaded with shopping and secrets some only
to be wrapped and opened while others remained
forever hidden behind the walls of the heart.
And children some laughing and some screaming
their voices merging until it was impossible to tell.

Now she sits and all day, hears from outside
the harsh bite of apple, the slow moan of traffic.

Incident at a Post Office Counter

I weighed the package for Dublin.
The teller scratched his memory.
'Dublin? Is that Northern or Southern?'

I reassured him. He pushed the stamps
With his palms towards me like a croupier.

Licking them I couldn't help wondering
If his weakness was Geography or History.

Naming

Pity the mule the unloved beast of the badlands
Breaking the day's fast on whins and thistles.

The product of the horse's lack of judgement
And the ass's snobbery and an open gate.

Neither fish nor flesh a stubborn loner
With a cock like a cudgel that can breed no children.

Inside the farm-keep young of all kinds thumb their
Noses. No solace either in the litany of plants

Around him. Dogrose, catnip, cowparsley, horseradish.
His soft heart trembles at the almost of mulberry.

Elves

Take nine gifted elves, a bit of cosmic
jiggerypokery and a womb to work in.

The first is an eye maker because that's how
it all starts. He takes inspiration from magazines.

The second fashions the lips pouting
into a mirror until he gets it just right.

The third is a neck elf, unnecked himself
he works from imagination and Japanese prints.

The fourth will make the breasts having watched
drops in slow motion fall into a basin of water.

The fifth oversees the area between milk and honey
laying down a flat surface with room for expansion.

The sixth is as private as an undertaker, folding
and tucking charged nerves deftly under membrane.

The seventh is an aromatherapist blending from
juniper and privet and mandrake and coral and radish.

The eight is a leglover. Finding feet pedestrian
he recalls soft-focus porn viewed from escalators.

The ninth designs the back. No great lover of Ingres,
he plants knuckles of vertebrae, blades of shoulder.

All nine leave contented, unaware that in the course
of nine human months many things change for the worse.

Palmer's Kiss

Unsure of the future we visited
a fortune teller (we have a house,
enough money and two children
at a private school). But still we wanted
to be sure our luck would hold.

She held court in a small kiosk
on the pier of a seaside town. It
was cold autumn and we breezed in
fresh in furs, the eyes on some still moist.

She hardly looked up from behind
her counter. A headscarf enveloped her
hair and a cat raised one ear at our greeting.

Unused to protocol (we knew how to
behave at dinner parties, funerals,
post-graduate dos and weddings.
But with a fortune teller?) – we knelt.

She glanced up, gold dangled from her ears,
pearls shone in her eyes, rubies clung to her lips.

She took my right in hers and with
one delicate finger slowly traced the lines.
Oh, the joy.

Miracle

On the last night of the wake, sitting alone
with the corpse and the candle and the stopped clock,

The wind shooing the light across the ceiling
and lapping the faces of the new dead in shadow.

The room is as quiet as mice and downstairs
the old watch sleeps in the hold of the house.

Outside, the June night is thick with conspiracies
of life under and on the ground and in the darting air.

You lie undisturbed, your hair sleeked back and
your skin unworried by the tremor of a vagrant nerve.

Love is too weak to wish any bit of the past undone
and when they wet their eyes and say you died too young

I know the past was best and love's deceit waits ahead
and I would turn Jesus, fresh from
the triumph of Lazarus, away from your bed.

'When it happens'

When it happens how will you kill
Your children? You could, being loving,
Cuddle them to death, planting big smackeroos
On their dead ears.

Or you could, being medical, overdose them
On chocolate drink, spooning the last dross
Like medicine down their juddering necks.

Or you could, being dramatic, shoot them
Cleanly through the forehead, deliberately
Missing the apple placed playfully on their heads.

Or you could, being military, put them against
A wall and shoot them after some stirring music
And a court martial where the evidence was never in doubt.

Or you could, being religious, crucify them
And then, full of remorse, take them down and rub
Oil of aloe into the crevices of their palms.

Or you could, being cowardly, stab them
In the back when they are looking out a window,
Then run into a darkened room and hide.

Being childless you have no excuse for inaction.
The orphanages are brimming. Go and kill them
In the old way, dispassionately.

Stalag

Last week from the closeness of our guarded
street a prisoner made a break for freedom.

She left in broad daylight without money or false
papers, disguised only in her best coat with lips
flared and rouge smeared in the hollows of her cheeks.

So audacious it took us all by surprise. We expected
flight by dust cart or dressed as a padre or a Red
Cross worker or the familiar uniform of the watch.

Old lags who groaned under the cosy ritual of camp
life clacked their tongues disapprovingly and others
who jogged daily or pressed weights faithfully in
the evening said she had chosen the wrong time.

At night when the stars burned at infinity
beyond the lampposts and the breeze breasted the curtains
we wondered where her body filled the hollow of some bed.

Of course she was caught and led back handcuffed
to her children, the door closed and the curtains shut.

She went before the Kommandant. What happened
is unclear but there were shouts and whimpering and a loss
of face. Later she emerged wearing dark glasses and
a roll neck, the kind we once used to hide love bites.

Closing Time

When the admirers have gone home
I feed the gibbon and the lion
Fruit and flesh bought at the corner shop.

The rhinoceros needs hay and the camel
Lips water prudently. The zebra
And the Polish horse relish the same mouthful.

The tiger feasts on the lamb and the puma
Licks blood from the armpit of the rabbit.

The antelope buries its snout in clover
And the caribou nibbles the pastures of dandelion.

I feed the crocodile on the softness of duck
And the pirhana on the necks of swans.

Snakes open their hinged mouths for a haunch of ox
And angelfish gulp the embalmed bodies of flies.

The bees are self-sufficient; the ants trim leaves
And wasps make paper for tomorrow's news.

Don't Ask

The bricklayer doesn't ask the brick
If it's comfortable there. If it lies snugly
Enough along the line and takes
The weight above it, it will do.

The roofer doesn't ask the tile if
It minds the weather. Cunning as survival
It casts the drop on the one below
Spreading the misery. The ground
Bulky and enough of it absorbs all.

The finished house doesn't ask the occupier
Who pays the bills or starts the arguments
Or whose turn it is to turn off the light.
It has learned its lesson and sits tight.

The spermatozoon doesn't ask the ovum who
Started the foreplay but gets down
To the business of geometric progression.
The finished baby lies like love on the carpet.

Ceremonies

I hate preliminaries,
grace before meals, lipping
the wine and smelling the cork,

Kissing before love-
making, small talk before kissing,
pregnancy before childbirth,
childhood before the real thing.

Arguing before the big bust-up,
manoeuvres before the shooting war.

I hate the bit players before
the main actor, the failed comedian
before the funny man, the chorus
girls before the stripper, the clown
before the tightrope walker,
the triple jump before the high wall,
the ball boys before the players,
the umpire before the bowler
and the damned music before everything.

Most of all I hate long drawn out
illness, praying and drugtaking,
mending and regressing, ingrown
tears and fake jollity

when one could simply drop
dead in the middle of something.

The Last Days of Jesus

It's hard knowing what's going to happen
To make any plans. He neglected the garden,
Saw the lawn creep on to the drive and let
The two pointed conifers wither in their tubs.

He knew he should be out healing the sick
Or knocking on doors preaching the word,
Or casting out devils, or feeding the poor.

He didn't go for drinks after work. A spoilsport,
They called him. Nor did he weave a part in the light
Fabric of conversation or plan the next year's outing.

The few evenings left to him he would stand
At the back gate smoking, looking over the fields
And watched the horizon darken before the falling sun
And the oaks spreading their arms in welcome.

First Reader

It is Funday, John and
Jane are in the park. They

Are sitting on the grass
Under some trees. Birds are.

The sun shines on the grass.
Bits of sun shine on John and Jane.

The day passes quickly, shadows
Come, the wind blows spots of cold.

Let's go now, said John. Yes
Let's go, said Jane. It is late.

There was much more they might
Have said but nobody could read it.

Old Customs

Our ancestors got dressed to kill.
A diversion against the drabness of a land
Of boggy places and water loving plants and no roads.

A break from the monogamy of the fixed place
Where only conversation dried up and
The high staggered trees let the evening in early.

Even love-making was irksome after a bit
When the poet and the druid and the chief
And the chief's son pulled all the best birds
With a bit of blarney or goddamned arrogance.

So when the war came they preened themselves
In Sunday best with woad and henna, their
Cheeks daubed; their eyes and lips flared with vanity.

Brides took a back seat at the mirror that day
As they plucked their eyebrows and puckered their lips
And flexed their pectorals (how they must have longed for cameras).

The battle itself was of course bloody awful.
Chests were opened like handbags
And more than mascara ran from gashes in the skull.

Unsure of the outcome the others waited on high ground,
The women practising kissing and keening by turns,
While the poet and the druid prepared for the worst and the best.

Mermaid

You say so little. A mermaid in a sealed cave
Gives more away. You watch me speak listening
With your whole face, the flow of my words entering
Through the pores of your skin. Nothing escapes.
Later you play it all back and find hidden messages.

You are the great confessor. You sit, your impassive,
Beautiful face intent, your eyes shielding your soul.
Only your generous moist lips slightly parted show
Where there is a way in. What I want is to speak through
Your tongue, to look out through your eyes, to know
Your blood washing around the soft tissues of my brain.

Only when you're angry do you revisit as a human.
Your deep eyes sharpen, you unlovely your face,
You let your articulate tongue lash the world. I
Flounder, then drown in the torrent of your blame.

At peace a mermaid, in anger and in love-
Making a fish wife.

Seaside Postcard

Tonight the vacancy in your heart is filled.
A tourist of love with his grubby suit-
Case and scented wash bag, having tramped
The rain brightened streets, saw the lit
Sign in your window signalling free space.

Our lodging was winter frozen in the lock
Hard year and in a street where few people
Moved and a house where nobody visits, silence
Passed as companionship between the stoic walls.

In spring when the birds thawed out of the early
Hedges, the tourists arrived, freeloaders
And one night opportunists. It was inevitable
That among the seaside landladies touting
One would find room enough in your small house.

Tomorrow morning there will be rings of laughter
In the kitchen, kippers coloured of gold and marmalade
Of onyx and best cups jangling like little bells.

You will prepare him a packed lunch and send him
Out warm with a kiss and a map of the town.
From early evening you will sit behind the door
Waiting, your heart sickening for his return.

Planning the Future

This is how it works. Imagine
What you want to be. Money;
Some in the bank, notes in your
Wallet, change in your trouser's pocket.

Women, one at a time will do,
Attracted by the money but settling
For the change and spoilt by a note
When you're feeling generous.

On holidays where they both meet
In her tan, you know you've made it.
Just pity the poor slobs on lilos
With their fat pale women and
Apartments with lino on the floor.

While they make love like walruses
You can feel superior glancing
Off each other like dolphins on silk.

All you need now to complete your joy
Is eternal life and the eternal danger of losing it.

Orpheus

Archway, an unlikely place to make myths.
True there is a way under ground and a flower
seller and a woman still missing. And music.

What does one do because it's still cold on earth?
Blow on your hands, walk about, have a cappuccino?
At least try not to look conspicuous and stood up.

The desire for spring and the need to please a mother
makes heroism inevitable. The long journey down
alone. Theatre adverts (one ironically advertising *Loot*)
paper over the cracks. Dogs must be carried. No music.

All day searching the same labyrinth and eating chocolate.
Finally the last train to Mill Hill opens its shut doors. No one.

Until in the far distance unmistakable, like a shadow
she alights cool as cucumber, enigmatic and fey.
Seeds germinating in her belly. Me at sixes and sevens.

A Short History

In the beginning one man killed
one man over some incident too trivial
to remember for more than a day.

Two men who knew that one man
slightly killed that one man who
himself had killed.

Four men who didn't particularly
like the one man but who liked the two men
less killed the two men who slew
the one man who himself had slain.

It grew; now eight thousand men
slaughtered four thousand men, but that was
over the ownership of a bull or the
white flanks of a queen.

Others joined in, carrying papal
bulls always ready to pull new scabs
off old wounds ready to heal.

So complicated now one would need a
textbook on genealogy to know who
to kill and who to look to for mercy.

Morning

You lie on your face naked and dead
to the world, one arm buried to the elbow
in the shadow of your hair, the other,
pale and meagre, follows the line of your body
downwards. The morning half light brightens
your shoulders and picks out the knuckles
on your vertebrae. I trace my eye down the line
to the dip where your back is forded in shadow.

This is a moment for silence, a takeout when
light and room and you and bed are one and I
am an intruder here, a leftover from the night.

I should go quietly now before the sun, wilful
and bossy, drives the shadows from the corners and
shows me inadequate and foolish standing at the door.

You rise in stages and sit on the bed confused
and clutch your hands protectively in your lap;
the night in your hair, your breasts indolent
and your bony hips square and flat on the mattress.

Caught between your night and daytime shape, you
look up yawning, wondering what the fuss is all about.

A Walk

Some day we'll walk alone in a wide field
keeping a safe distance. You downwind.

The gale sweeping away any trace of you
into the scutched hedges. Even your voice

caught on a tongue of wind will be carried out
there where the phone lines zing and tremble.

The patch of face visible between your high
collar and unruly hair has the colour of drained sky.

Looking out over the long farmland I'd say
'This is a day to break promises.'

You say nothing, pushing back the chiffon
which caresses your face like an afterthought.

Rescuing a Puppy

Early in the New Year you may find a puppy
dumped from a speeding car where the city meets
the trees exposed when the wind flattens the grass.

Take him in your arms and run home panting past
beggars and street hawkers and sellers of magazines,
past drunks, some truculent and some past truculence,
past the temporarily insane and those far into madness,

Past a high car park where a lone suicide pumps
courage into her lungs before the long
fall from grace, past houses where some children sleep
and where some silently endure the ritual of desire.

Run past the hospital where the absent minded
professors of dementia pad from ward to ward
in their socks searching, where the too young
to die meet the too old to live, while the rest
play nurses and doctors all day and all night long.

Once inside take a duvet from your bed.
Nest it near a radiator to warm his little body.
Place him gently on it putting your ear to his ribcage

Prepare a bottle of full cream milk, skin warm
and knock the neighbouring doors for disused teats
explaining why. Then nurse him, an all night vigil,
reinventing (if your Latin is up to it) the mantra
Catullus dei qui tollis peccata mundi, until dawn.

Frieze in the British Museum

You had eyes only for the lions. Some
squaring up to kings and some pierced
from shoulder to haunch, weeping stone.

Such an unequal battle, the carved manes
swept back, their heads noble like sphinxes
and the digits of their great paws big as forearms.

You watched with your immeasurably sad eyes
murmuring as if for the loss of children and as if
your pity alone would bring them back to life.

The straggled line of captive men pleading and begging
with all the gestures of hopeless fear in the face
of pitiless and arrogant authority, a pre-run of what
we learned to do much better, would make stones weep.

But it was the lions that won your heart that day
in the long gallery. I could feel your hand colden and
your fingers, so tiny to those digits, bite my palm with little nails.

Love's Alchemist

You are love's alchemist. You
read the hedges as we take
the gathering evening in our stride.

Above us unseen stars fill the sky with
messages too subtle for my untrained eye.

I stoop to kiss and own your lips while
your hands read the phrenology of my skull.

Indoors your kitchen is ringed with charms,
jars of dried leaves, canisters of seedlings,
sprigs preserved half-green on the withering
point; the fragrance of thyme, the short cud
of rosemary, sage sharpening the tongue.

And finally the comfits, modest aconite and
wayward belladonna for simulated flight,
until stinging hot tea from the resentful
nettle brings us back to earth.

Reassurance of Hands

On a bright autumn night, the moon blanched
almond and the fruits of the wide sky hanging
from the trees of Asgard, she walks in the garden,
more lovely than night and more drained than shadow.

Around her the early returns of the day's heat fall
like broken promises on the spread lap of the earth.

She counts her fingers to reassure herself of a single
constancy, the sureness of small jointed bones that
can unpick frayed thread, can tease perfume out of
thorns of rosemary, can number vertebrae in the dark.

She holds her face with her hands at an angle. The sharp
pins of stars peering into the crevices around her eyes. If
another holding the same face, pointing it at the busy
night and searching with the same eagerness of forgiving
love the lines of passion taut and fit to burst, he would fall

to her knees and gathering her hips into his companionship
hold her for as long as the night can hold its breath.

She would cry but that is such an abuse of a night's stillness.
What's gone is well gone and can't be tugged back and
chastened like an unruly dog straining on a new scent. And

far beyond her in the north sky receding gods; the faint
sound of horses and meadhalls with dust and lost music in the lofts.

Nightfears

The ghosts of some nights come back on some nights
and, without as much as by your leave, sit on their usual
side of the sofa. Pretend you haven't seen them, they

ruffle the nape of your neck with small skilled fingers.
Your back tightens and your hand on the remote control
mutes all sound. They are back to stay for as long as it takes
for you to face your past and admit it was worth it.

They bring with them neither the smell of evening nor of earth
but the clean sultriness of sun caged between trees, of orchards
dipping and of the morning before the wet melts from fields.

That is the terror they bring. We have learned to deal with others,
death by wire, acres of skulls, bodies on flame, long lines of rotund
corpses on stilts of bones, children their teeth grinding in some
horror
before the night ends and the first buses run and the dogs stir.

We can neutralise these. Press the mute into life and listen to the
sweet
sounds of life exploding, colour deafening your eyes and passion
itself,
sounding somewhere between surprise and fear, tickling your back.

But you with silent parted lips, your face in shade and the V-light
on your neck, you with the open secrets of your body, your delicate
bones,
bring the one terror we must not entertain; that we might find
life once held close and kissed almost to death too beautiful to leave
behind.

On Solving Problems

We were always careful, the boat waiting,
tied up, caulked and the oars shipped.

You with your clipboard.

A military operation. First the goose
all white and gold was rowed across
riding the prow like Cleopatra.

Next the fox smelling dangerously herded
by your stick into the hold; all nose
and eyes and cunning little paws.

I take the goose back confused but hopeful.
You tick her off the list and point to the corn.

I lift the sheaf and row holding it
between my knees to where the fox sulks.

Back for the goose, you swimming the final
journey like a dolphin mesmerised by the wake.

Always so careful I think it's about time
we broke the bloody rules. Let the fox
loose on the goose and the goose loose
on the corn. Where one dies another is born.

The goose's terror shakes the hard seed free
which the fox plants with unwanted meat carelessly.

Survey while you can this botched place,
a halm of gold corn around your neck,
blood specks on your face.

Oedipus Shopping

Oedipus they said had one eye too many. He took the
fool's way stabbing the light out with a blunt needle.
That's that then. I'll never see her again or Thebes
Or the palace or the arched bed or the flower garden
Or hair falling in light or dawn cracking the windowpane.

Now with all the freedom in the world he shops alone
in supermarkets, manoeuvring a stubborn trolley.
The cluster of lettuce reminds him damnably of something
else. The nipple of cantaloupe catches his breath. A pineapple
is an argument carried into bed before the skin sheds itself.
He kisses in a nectarine the freshness of her mouth.

Tiresias works on the cold meat counter, doling out
measures of brawn and olives and entrails and tongue.

The bread smells homely, kitchens of risen loaf, whole
wheat and soup, butter melting on the edges of morning.
Wine. He asked for red, her favourite colour, the neck
slender to the shoulders waiting to be opened, new and surprising.

There is no escape from enchantment. The heart knows that.
The gesture was theatrical and only meant to impress.

The Autism of Pigs

On a wet day in March, smurr and muck in the farmyard.
The pigs waiting for the hatchet man flapped their ears,
Like the first birds caught between experimentation and hope.

Imagine their surprise when the down current caught
their pink bodies in its arms and wafted them
into the air. Like Jesus in his ascension or Disney playing
with imagination they spread and shook earth from their cloots
and let the day's currents wheel them in the circle of light.

It's all about belief when your bumble bee body questions
gravity. They flew, ears like jumbo and their trotters at right
angles to the ground, their curly wurly tails pointing
straight back at where they came from. They filled their lungs
and moved their slow heads like raptors curious and alone.

Below the land of dreams pricked their conscience, buildings
with arrows of desire or crosses marking a spot. Bridges
walked across the river at random, ropes holding turrets in a grip
of steel. Oh the autism of pigs. No detail escaped
their unrelenting eyes. Lovers in a park went in and caressed in the
soft palate of their brains. The homeless sat motionless
and angry in their stony memory. The mad went in their nostrils
and huddled between the crowded spaces and the need for peace.
The lonely walked down the dried riverbeds of their hemispheres
looking for conversation or a light or the time of day.

Below the accusing fingers pointing heavenwards, a Nuremberg
of hands raised in anger when the unwanted float out of reach.
There was nothing for it but a crash landing as near Smithfields
as possible and let the hatchet men cut to the quick. Boiled tongue
muted, back rasher, leg and shoulder surrendered, soft liver dived
through fingers. Only the head with the forbidden apple faced the
                                                              front

and of course the tired eyes remembering and accepting almost
                                                        everything.